CUBA

BY EDMUND LINDOP

FRANKLIN WATTS
New York/London/Toronto/Sydney/1980
A FIRST BOOK

FRONTISPIECE: MORRO CASTLE WAS BUILT BY THE
SPANISH IN THE LATE 1500s, TO PROTECT THE PORT OF HAVANA.
IT IS TODAY ONE OF CUBA'S BEST-KNOWN LANDMARKS.

Photographs courtesy of: Grolier, Inc.: frontispiece, pp.
6, 47, 48, 55; The New York Public Library Picture
Collection: p. 17; Paula DiPerna: p. 22; Wide World
Photos, Inc.: pp. 39, 40.

Map on page 5 by Vantage Art, Inc.

Cover photograph by Paula DiPerna.

Library of Congress Cataloging in Publication Data

Lindop, Edmund.
Cuba.

(A First book)
Bibliography: p.
Includes index.
SUMMARY: A history of Cuba including a discussion of
the way of life today in that now-Communist country.
1. Cuba—History—Juvenile literature.
[1. Cuba—History] I. Title.
F1758.5.L56   927.91   79–24010
ISBN 0–531–04101–8

CONTENTS

For Esther and Laurie Lindop

PEARL OF THE ANTILLES

In October of 1492, just two weeks after he first sighted land in the New World, Christopher Columbus sailed to the northeastern coast of Cuba. Columbus and the Spanish sailors waded ashore, eager to explore this new land that lay before them.

The first glimpse of Cuba delighted the weary sailors who had spent nearly three long months aboard their small ships. Sparkling blue waves lapped softly against white sandy beaches and coral reefs. Tall stately palm trees waved gently in the breeze. A lush green grassland stretched as far as the eye could see. In the midst of the grassland were fruit trees, brilliant flowers, and a variety of beautiful birds. Truly this was a tropical paradise. No wonder Columbus wrote in his journal that he had found "the most beautiful land that human eyes have ever seen."

Columbus was convinced that this land was part of Asia. He believed that when he sailed west from Spain he would reach India and the rich region of China that Marco Polo had visited. This is why he called the islands of the Caribbean Sea the "Indies" and the people who lived there "Indians."

The sailors met natives in Cuba who wore gold nuggets as

ornaments. So Columbus was even more certain that he was near the land of gold, spices, and precious stones—the land ruled by the emperor of China. For more than a month the explorers hunted in Cuba for the treasure-filled places that Marco Polo had described. Columbus even sent messengers inland with gifts and letters for the Chinese emperor.

But the explorer who discovered Cuba never found the riches he was seeking. And he never realized that Cuba was the most important island in the New World.

At the top of Cuba's coat of arms is a golden key suspended between two points of land. These two points of land are Florida and the Yucatán Peninsula of Mexico. Cuba, which is the golden key, lies between these two lands. It is only about 90 miles (145 km) south of Florida and about 130 miles (209 km) northeast of Mexico.

Cuba is near the northern end of the long chain of islands called the West Indies. This island chain, which is about 2,000 miles (3,220 km) long, stretches almost all the way from Florida to Venezuela, and it separates the Caribbean Sea from the Atlantic Ocean.

The four largest islands in the West Indies—Cuba, Hispaniola (Haiti and the Dominican Republic), Jamaica, and Puerto Rico—are known as the Greater Antilles. (The name *Antilia* was given by early geographers to a fabled island of great treasures that lay "somewhere across the sea.") Beautiful Cuba has often been called the Pearl of the Antilles.

THE LAND

During prehistoric times Cuba was part of an underwater mountain range that connected North America to South America. Then, many millions of years ago, Cuba was raised from the seafloor by volcanic action. So the island of Cuba is really the peak of an underwater mountain.

Cuba is almost as large as all the other West Indian islands combined. Actually, Cuba consists of one large island and more than 1,600 smaller ones. Most of these other islands are tiny, and only a few have people living on them. One, however, is larger than the others and has a population of about 30,000 people. It is the Isle of Pines, about 40 miles (64 km) south of the main island of Cuba. The Isle of Pines is believed to have been the setting for Robert Louis Stevenson's famous adventure story, *Treasure Island*.

The shape of Cuba is sometimes said to look like an alligator. The island is much longer than it is wide. From east to west it extends almost 750 miles (1,207 km). But most of the island has a breadth of about 60 miles (96 km), and even the widest section is only 120 miles (193 km) across.

Almost three-quarters of Cuba's land is either level or has gently rolling slopes. Much of this land was once covered with limestone. During a period of many centuries the limestone weathered into a deep layer of dark red clay. This rich clay provides an excellent soil for growing a wide variety of crops.

The three highland areas in Cuba are widely separated. The highest mountains are the Sierra Maestra near the southeastern coast. Some peaks here rise more than 6,000 feet (9,660 km) above sea level. The Sierra de Trinidad in central Cuba is a lower mountain rage. The western highlands, called the Sierra de los Organos, have limestone formations that have weathered into unusual shapes. Some are lumpy hills that look like haystacks. Others are limestone columns resembling organ-pipes, which give the Sierra de los Organos its name.

Cuba's long coastline is indented by some of the best ports in the world. Many of the 200 ports are shaped like bottles with narrow entrances that broaden into spacious deepwater bays. The narrow entrances protect ships anchored in the bays against waves and wind. Through the centuries many trading ships, pirate vessels, and warships have stopped at Cuba's fine ports.

There are about 200 rivers in Cuba, but nearly all of them are short, narrow, and too shallow for ships. The Cauto is the longest river, and it winds through the southeastern part of the island for about 150 miles (241 km). But only about half of this distance can be navigated.

THE CLIMATE

The weather in Cuba is pleasantly warm the year round. Although Cuba lies within the tropics, the surrounding bodies of water and the trade winds give it a mild climate. The average temperature is about 70°F. (21°C.) in the winter and about 80°F. (27°C.) in the summer.

Cuba has a rainy season and a dry season. The wet season is from May to October, when thunderstorms occur frequently. During the rest of the year there is little rain. This pattern of rainfall is good for growing sugarcane and other crops. The sugarcane receives plenty of moisture while it is growing and can be harvested during the dry season. The average yearly rainfall is 54 inches (137 cm). Some years, however, Cuba receives much less rain. During these periods of drought crops are poor and livestock suffer severely.

Like other Caribbean islands, Cuba lies in the path of destructive windstorms called hurricanes. The hurricane season usually lasts from August to October. Huge masses of hot air gather above the ocean and swirl around and around at speeds often greater than 100 miles (161 km) an hour. When these revolving air masses move forward they can strike mighty blows at both people and property.

THE PEOPLE

Cuba has a population of nearly 10 million people. It has more people than any other island in the West Indies.

Although Cuba is chiefly an agricultural country, only about two out of every five Cubans live in rural areas. Most people live in the cities and towns. Nearly 2 million people live in Havana, the capital and largest city. This means that about one-fifth of all Cubans reside in the capital city and its suburbs.

Except for Havana, Cuba has no other very big cities. Santiago de Cuba, on the southeastern coast, has about 300,000 people. Camagüey, in central Cuba, has about 200,000 people. Three other cities have a population of over 100,000, and thirty-five towns have between 10,000 and 100,000 inhabitants.

About three-quarters of the Cubans are white, mainly of Spanish descent. Most of the rest are black or *mulatto* (persons of mixed black and white ancestry). Long ago Cuba also had a large Indian population, but today only a few Indians remain.

EARLY DAYS

At the time of Columbus' arrival, Cuba was inhabited by the Taíno and Ciboney peoples. Both of these Indian groups probably came from South America. The Ciboneys reached Cuba first, but by 1492, the Taínos were the larger and dominant group.

The Taínos were peaceful Stone Age people who fished, hunted, and farmed for food. They lived in small villages and were divided into clans, each headed by a chief. Their homes were circular huts made of wooden poles with cone-shaped roofs of palm leaves. From cotton that grew wild on the island they made hammocks for sleeping and thread for fishlines and nets. Their fishhooks were made from animal horns, and their harpoons were tipped with sharp bones.

For fishing, the Taínos used canoes hollowed out from cedar logs and powered by oars. The canoes provided transportation along the coasts of Cuba and across the sea to other islands. Some canoes were large enough to hold eighty passengers.

On their farms the Taínos grew *maize* (Indian corn), potatoes, beans, peppers, and a root called *cassava*, which they baked as a kind of bread. The Taínos smoked tobacco leaves rolled into the shape of cigars. When some of the Indians gathered, one in the group carried a big cigar and a lighted torch. Now and then he lit the cigar, and everyone took a puff.

ENTER THE SPANIARDS

Nearly twenty years elapsed between the time Columbus discovered Cuba and the founding of the first Spanish settlement on the island. This was because the Spaniards first turned their attention to colonizing the adjacent island of Hispaniola. Finally, in 1511, Diego Velasquez, the wealthiest planter in Hispaniola, landed in Cuba and established a colony at Baracoa. By 1515, seven towns, including Havana, had been started on the island.

The prospect of finding gold attracted the first white settlers to Cuba. They enslaved the Taínos, forcing them to pan the rivers for gold and work in the few mines that were discovered. Working underground in the mines, the Indians had to breathe stale air and face the danger of being trapped if the mine collapsed. Many could not stand the backbreaking toil day after day. Large numbers of them became ill and died.

If the overworked Indians complained, they often were beaten or tortured. And they had no resistance to the white man's diseases. The Indians picked up infections that proved fatal to them but not to the Spaniards. "Their only weapon was flight," wrote Father Las Casas, a priest and historian, who observed how the Indians suffered in Cuba. "I have seen cruelty there," he said sadly, "that no living man has ever seen, nor could imagine ever seeing."

We don't know for certain how many Indians lived in Cuba when the Spaniards arrived. Some estimates say there may have been 200,000 Indians. But only fifty years after the Spanish invasion, only about 5,000 scattered Indians remained.

For more than two centuries the population and economy of Cuba grew very slowly. During those years the island's chief importance was its strategic location guarding the entrance to the Gulf of Mexico. Large merchant fleets would stop at Havana, where the ships were divided into two groups. One group went to Mexico and the other to Panama. On their return voyage the trading vessels reunited at Havana before crossing the ocean.

To protect the port of Havana the Spanish built three strong forts. The largest of these was Morro Castle, which overlooks the port entrance. Built in the late 1500s, Morro Castle is still Cuba's best known landmark and greatest tourist attraction.

BLACK WORKERS
AND
THE SUGAR BOOM

The economy of Cuba changed dramatically in the late 1700s. In 1762 the British seized Havana. They held the city for less than a year, but during that time the British greatly increased trade between Cuba and their colonies in North America. The chief product that the American colonists wanted from nearby Cuba was sugar. This American market for Cuban sugar grew even larger after the Revolutionary War.

For many years the people of Europe had received much of their sugar from Hispaniola. But slave revolts in Hispaniola, which began in 1791, led to a long period of warfare that damaged the island's sugar industry. So the Europeans, like the Americans, began looking to Cuba to supply them with sugar.

Before the Spanish planters in Cuba could provide all the sugar that was needed, they had to greatly expand their work force. Since the Indians had been almost eliminated, the planters began importing large numbers of black slaves from Africa.

(10)

Black slaves were not new to Cuba; the first Africans had been brought to the island in 1517. But the number of blacks coming to Cuba before 1790 was only a small trickle compared with the huge torrent that arrived with the sugar boom. By 1825, the black people in Cuba outnumbered the whites, and twenty years later the island had nearly 900,000 blacks and fewer than 600,000 whites.

UNITED STATES INTEREST IN CUBA GROWS

Ever since the days when Thomas Jefferson was President, Americans had wanted to acquire the valuable island that lies so near the United States. Southerners were especially eager to have the United States annex Cuba because they felt it could become another slave state.

During the 1840s and 1850s, the American Presidents, James K. Polk, Franklin Pierce, and James Buchanan all tried to buy Cuba from Spain. In 1848, the United States made an offer of $100 million; by 1854 the amount was raised to $130 million. But Spain refused to sell the island.

The desire to annex Cuba as another slave state died with the Civil War and the freeing of slaves. American interest in Cuba, however, continued to grow. Businessmen from the United States began investing heavily in the Cuban sugar industry. American companies started buying land and combining the smaller sugar farms into large plantations. They built new sugar mills, office buildings, and railroad tracks that connected the canefields to mills and ports. By the 1890s United States investments on the island were valued at about $50 million. Yankee influence on the Cuban economy was growing stronger with each passing year.

(11)

A CENTURY
OF TURMOIL

For three centuries Spain owned the largest and richest empire in the Americas. But, between 1808 and 1825, all of Spain's mainland colonies, from Mexico in the north to Argentina and Chile in the south, revolted against Spanish rule and set up independent governments. The once-dazzling Spanish empire was reduced to two Caribbean islands—Cuba and Puerto Rico.

Spain was determined to hold onto Cuba at any cost. Huge Spanish armies were stationed on the island to maintain close control over the people. Spanish governors ruled Cuba as tight-fisted dictators. They would not allow the people to hold elections or to attend political meetings, and one governor even forbade Cubans to read newspapers or books in public places. The people were heavily taxed, while government officials made personal fortunes through bribery and other forms of corruption.

Nearly all the important positions in the Cuban government were held by Spanish-born white persons. Yet many of Cuba's best educated citizens—lawyers, teachers, plantation owners, and business people—had been born on the island. They were called *Creoles* (persons of Spanish ancestry born in the

New World). These Creoles became increasingly unhappy because the important government jobs went to the newly arrived Spaniards instead of to native-born Cubans.

Most of the peasants in Cuba lived in miserable poverty. They had little food and shabby clothing. They lived in crowded shacks with earth floors and no windows. Usually they did not have any education or medical care. Nearly a million of these poor people were black slaves.

Conditions were ripe for revolution in Cuba. In October 1868, Carlos Manuel de Céspedes, a wealthy Creole planter, joined with thirty-seven other planters to proclaim the *Grito de Yara* (the cry of Yara, a town near Céspedes' plantation). This was a declaration of war against Spanish rule. Céspedes and his planter comrades then freed their slaves, who joined in the rebellion for Cuban independence.

Over a period of several years the Cubans won some spectacular victories, and, at one time, they controlled about half of the island. But the Spanish government, angered by the rebels' gains, finally sent enough troops to crush the rebellion. The war ended in 1878 with the surrender of the Cuban patriots. It had lasted a full decade—which is why it was called the Ten Years' War—resulting in the loss of over 250,000 lives and the destruction of thousands of acres of crops. In the peace treaty, the Spanish government promised to improve conditions in Cuba and to gradually abolish slavery on the island. Finally, in 1886, the slaves were freed. But the Spanish leaders made no other reforms in Cuba.

Cuba Libre! (Free Cuba) became the rallying cry for another revolt that began in 1895. More and more Cubans were growing disgusted with Spanish tyranny and taxation, and joined the movement for independence.

One of the leaders of this movement was a poet and journalist, José Martí. At the age of sixteen he had been imprisoned for speaking out against Spanish rule. After his release from prison, he was deported and warned never to return to his native land. But Martí was determined that Cuba be freed from Spanish oppression. Moreover, he felt that Cuba must be completely independent and not fall under the political or economic control of the United States.

In New York City Martí worked with other exiles to collect funds and weapons for a full-scale revolution in Cuba. In February 1895, uprisings occurred on the island, and a short time later Martí secretly landed on a Cuban beach. Although he was not a trained soldier and his health was poor, Martí insisted on fighting alongside the other rebels. On May 19, 1895, while riding to a battle, he was killed by a Spanish sniper.

The fallen martyr became Cuba's greatest hero. Today, throughout the island there are many statues of the "Father of freedom," and the highest award that can be given by the Cuban government is the José Martí Medal.

As the rebellion spread throughout the island, the Spanish army was reinforced by 200,000 additional troops. Their new commander, General Valeriano Weyler, was tough and stern. He guessed correctly that many Cubans were sneaking guns, food, and medicine to the rebel forces. So General Weyler's soldiers built concentration camps into which they herded large numbers of men, women, and children. Living conditions in these camps were horrible, and thousands of Cubans died there from disease and starvation.

THE SPANISH-AMERICAN WAR

People in the United States learned about the dreadful conditions in Cuba from newspaper stories. Many Americans, shocked by the cruel treatment of Cubans in concentration camps, echoed the cry, "Cuba Libre!"

Fearing that the revolution in Cuba might threaten American lives and property, the United States government sent the battleship *Maine* to Havana. On February 15, 1898, a mysterious explosion destroyed the *Maine* and killed over 260 American sailors. Even today no one knows for sure how the explosion occurred. Probably the Spanish did not start it, since they did not want a war against the United States, with its superior military forces. Spain apologized to the United States for the incident. The Spanish government also promised to close the concentration camps and to give the Cubans a larger role in governing themselves.

But an angry American public and Congress blamed the Spanish for blowing up the *Maine,* and this was the spark that led to a declaration of war against Spain.

Responding to the slogan, "Remember the *Maine!*" thousands of Americans volunteered for armed service. The best known group of volunteers was the "Rough Riders," a cavalry unit led into battle by Theodore Roosevelt.

The war lasted less than four months. On both land and sea the Americans easily conquered the Spanish forces. By the peace treaty that ended this war, the United States was given the Spanish possessions of Puerto Rico, the Philippine Islands, and Guam. Cuba also was taken from Spain, but it did not become a United States possession.

THE PLATT AMENDMENT AND CUBAN INDEPENDENCE

The United States put its own military officers in control of Cuba until the people there could form their own democratic government. However, the United States refused to let the island become an independent nation until the Cubans agreed to include certain provisions in their constitution. These provisions were known as the Platt Amendment. (They were a series of conditions dealing with Cuba that had been introduced in the U.S. Congress by Senator Orville Platt.)

One provision of the Platt Amendment gave the United States the right to intervene in Cuban affairs whenever it felt such action was necessary to maintain Cuban independence or protect United States interests. Another provision allowed the United States to lease land in Cuba for military bases. That is how the United States acquired its important naval base at Guantánamo Bay in the southeastern part of the island.

The Cuban people resented the Platt Amendment, since it made their new nation almost a puppet of the United States. But they reluctantly accepted it because otherwise they would have had no government of their own. (Many years later, in 1934, the United States cancelled the Platt Amendment, except the provision to keep the Guantánamo Bay Naval Base.)

Elections were held in Cuba in 1901 for a president and congress. The voters elected Tómas Estrada Palma as their first president. On May 20, 1902, the United States flag was lowered in front of the governor's palace; in its place the flag of the new Republic of Cuba was raised.

Estrada Palma tried to govern Cuba wisely, but he faced strong opposition from power-hungry politicians and military officers. When he ran for reelection, his opponents charged that the election had been dishonest. Fighting broke out, and Estrada Palma asked the United States to intervene in order to avoid a civil war. In 1906, Estrada Palma resigned from the presidency, and for the next three years Cuba again was governed by officers sent from the United States.

Colonel Theodore Roosevelt led his calvery unit,
known as the "Rough Riders," into
Santiago de Cuba during the Spanish-American War.

The Second Republic of Cuba was established after American forces left the island in 1909. But in the years that followed, Cuba failed to achieve democracy. Elections often were dishonest and sometimes marked by violence and bloodshed. Presidents, congressmen, and other officeholders frequently were more concerned about making personal fortunes than they were about governing the country democratically. Meanwhile, the problems of the Cuban people were generally neglected, and many continued to live in wretched poverty.

Fulgencio Batista emerged as Cuba's most powerful political leader in the period between 1933 and 1958. During part of that time he ruled from behind the scenes through a series of "puppet" presidents. From 1940 to 1944 and again from 1952 to 1958 Batista himself was the head of the government.

Batista encouraged United States businesses to invest heavily in Cuba. By the late 1950s American firms controlled about 40 percent of the Cuban sugar industry, half of the island's trains, and 90 percent of the public utilities, such as electric power and telephones. American money also went into other Cuban industries, including tobacco, ranching, and oil refining.

The United States government regarded Batista as a friend who welcomed American business interests and maintained order in his country. But a growing number of people in both Cuba and the United States did not look upon Batista as a model president. This was partly because Batista used his office to provide himself with a huge fortune. (When he finally fled Cuba in 1958, it was estimated that Batista took with him between $300 million and $400 million.) Batista was criticized also because he largely ignored the needs of his people for schools, health care, and, above all, decent-paying jobs. But the worst charge against Batista was that he ruled, especially after

1952, as a brutal, ruthless dictator. His henchmen were said to have murdered over 20,000 Cubans who dared to oppose him.

As the terror spread across the island, Cubans who had cheered Batista in earlier years secretly plotted to overthrow him. University students rioted in the streets, revolts broke out in the army, and a plan to assassinate Batista almost succeeded. In towns throughout the land, rebels gathered strength and looked forward to the day when the cruel dictatorship would be ended.

CASTRO COMES
TO POWER

Fidel Castro was born on August 23, 1926, on his father's sugar plantation in the Cuban province (state) of Oriente. His parents were fairly wealthy, and they sent Fidel to Catholic schools. In school he was a good student and an excellent athlete. Powerfully built and over 6 feet (2 m) tall, Fidel was an outstanding baseball and basketball player and a superior track star.

At the age of nineteen Castro entered the law school at the University of Havana. There he became deeply involved with radical political groups. He was active in student riots and demonstrations that got him in trouble with the police.

After graduating from the law school, Castro began his career as an attorney and politician. He was a candidate for Congress in 1952 at the same time that former President Batista was running again for the presidency. Shortly before the election, Batista figured that he probably would not win. So instead of risking the chance that he might lose at the polls, Batista staged a revolt and overthrew the government. Then he suspended the elections for all other offices.

When Castro learned that he could not run for Congress, he was furious. He went before the Supreme Court and de-

cruited by Castro and trained in guerrilla warfare. Funds were collected from people in Latin America and the United States who wanted to see Batista driven from power. Castro used twelve thousand dollars of this money to purchase an old yacht called the *Granma*. Finally, in November 1956, the *Granma* left the Mexican coast and headed for Cuba. Eighty-two men were squeezed into a space built for eight passengers. After seven stormy days at sea, the *Granma* landed in southeastern Cuba.

Batista's spies had found out about the expedition, and his troops were waiting for the invaders when they arrived. Nearly all of the rebels were killed or captured. Only twelve, including the Castro brothers and Guevara, escaped the ambush and went into hiding in the Sierra Maestra mountain range.

The tiny band of tired, frightened rebels had only a few guns, no ammunition, and practically no food. The first few days they lived mainly on sugarcane that they cut from the ground in the mountain valleys. These twelve survivors were discouraged and some were ill, but they still were determined to achieve the miracle of winning the Revolution.

The Cuban government falsely announced that all of the rebels, including Fidel Castro, had been killed or captured. Three months passed before the Cuban people knew that a revolution had begun in the mountains near the eastern end of the island. The true story that Castro and his movement were still alive was finally revealed by a reporter from *The New York Times,* who visited the rebels in their mountain hideout.

Slowly the guerrilla band rallied support. Nearby farmers began believing that Castro's struggle was their struggle. They

*A mural of Che Guevara
at the Plaza de
la Revolucion in Havana.*

(23)

started bringing the rebels food, stolen guns, and ammunition. Cuban men and women joined the "26th of July Movement" at first by the dozens, later by the thousands.

The guerrilla fighters ambushed Batista's troops in cleverly concealed traps. They cut communication lines, seized trains carrying arms, bombed army supply posts, and started fires in canefields and sugar mills. Whenever Batista's forces suffered setbacks, he punished the Cuban people with more arrests, more executions, and more terrorism. Each time he did this, more Cubans went over to Castro's side. Even some soldiers in Batista's army deserted and started fighting for Castro.

In the final months of 1958 the course of the war moved rapidly toward total victory for the rebels. Castro's army had seized most of the rural areas and towns in three eastern provinces. When Santa Clara, a city near the middle of the island, fell on December 31, Batista knew he had lost the war. Instead of celebrating that New Year's Eve, he slipped out of Havana and took a plane to the Dominican Republic.

Fighting ceased after the rebel troops took over Santiago de Cuba on January 2, 1959. Then Castro began a week-long triumphant tour across the whole length of the island. At every stop he was greeted by cheering crowds, anxious to catch a glimpse of the bearded warrior. Finally, on January 8, riding on the top of a captured tank and wearing his wrinkled army pants and shirt, the conquering hero arrived in Havana.

Fidel Castro had come to the capital city of Cuba to end one revolution and start another. At first Castro seemed to have no definite plans for the kind of government he wanted in Cuba. He even waited a few months before giving himself the position of prime minister in the new government. Before long, however, it became evident that Castro was turning Cuba into a Communist country.

CUBA AND THE WORLD IN THE 1960s

In the first few months of Castro's new government, Cuba and the United States eyed each other suspiciously. Castro had some logical reasons for resenting the powerful country to the north. Throughout most of his struggle against Batista, the United States had supplied his enemy with aircraft, tanks, guns, and ammunition. Moreover, Castro wanted to end Cuba's economic dependence on the United States. For many years Cuba had bought about 80 percent of its imports from the United States. And a large share of nearly every major industry in Cuba was owned by American companies. Castro claimed that the United States treated Cuba as its colony and had a stranglehold on the island's economy.

Also, the new leader of Cuba was angry because the United States still clung to a valuable piece of Cuban property —the naval base at Guantánamo Bay, which he demanded that the United States return to Cuba.

People in the United States wondered about Cuba's future under the rule of the former guerrilla fighter. Castro promised that his Revolution would bring sweeping changes to Cuba—to its economy, government, and to the way of life for its people. Although in 1959 and 1960 Castro denied that he was a Communist, some observers claimed that his actions spoke louder than his words. His soldiers rounded up many of his enemies, and they were charged with committing crimes against the Revolution. They were given swift trials. Some were sentenced to prison; others were publicly executed. Journalists and members of Congress in the United States condemned Castro's "blood bath," claiming that his brutal treatment of enemies was similar to the way Russia disposed of its dissenters.

In May 1959, only four months after he came to power, Castro made his first major change in the country's economy. Under the First Agrarian Reform Law many huge farms in Cuba were broken up. Nearly 9 million acres (3.6 million hectares) of land, some belonging to United States companies, were seized by the Cuban government.

In 1960, relations between Cuba and the United States worsened when Castro ordered that the oil refineries on the island, which were American-owned, must refine oil that Cuba was obtaining from the Soviet Union. The oil companies refused to do this, so Castro seized the refineries.

The United States struck back by announcing in July 1960, that it was cutting by 95 percent the amount of sugar it normally bought from Cuba. Later that year the United States took an even more drastic step—it put an *embargo,* or halt, on all trade with Cuba. Castro retaliated by taking over all the remaining United States businesses in Cuba.

On January 2, 1961, Castro charged that most of the employees in the U.S. Embassy in Havana were spies, and he demanded that the United States withdraw seventy-six of its eighty-seven staff members within forty-eight hours. The following day an angry United States government ended all of its diplomatic relations with Cuba.

The island's economy was severely crippled when the United States ended all trade with Cuba. But during the same year, Cuba made a major trade agreement with the Soviet Union. In 1960, the Russians promised that they would buy one million tons of Cuban sugar annually for the next five years. In return Cuba would receive oil, machinery, wheat, and other Soviet products, plus a loan of $100 million for the purchase of industrial equipment. This agreement between Cuba and the Soviet Union caused many Americans to conclude that the island was becoming a close ally of Russia.

THE PLOT
TO OVERTHROW
CASTRO

Many Cubans escaped from their homeland when Castro came to power. Some fled Cuba because their businesses and properties were taken over by the new regime. After it became clear that Cuba was being turned into a Communist state, large numbers of doctors, lawyers, writers, professors, engineers, and skilled workers departed instead of being forced to work for the new government.

Over 600,000 Cuban refugees went to the United States, and smaller groups of exiles went to Spain and Latin American countries. About 500,000 Cuban exiles settled in or near Miami, Florida. Today more than one half of the population of Greater Miami is Cuban.

Some of the exiles were so determined to crush Castro's rule that they were willing to risk their lives for the cause. These exiles volunteered to take part in an armed invasion of their homeland. The Central Intelligence Agency, which is the branch of the United States government that directs undercover operations, developed a plan for the exiles' invasion of Cuba. In the spring of 1960, President Dwight D. Eisenhower approved the CIA's invasion plan.

The exile volunteers were sent to army camps in the Central American country of Guatemala. There they were secretly trained in guerrilla warfare by officers in the United States armed forces. For many months the men drilled at the maneuvers needed to invade and conquer their island homeland.

In January 1961, John F. Kennedy succeeded Eisenhower as President. Three months later the CIA informed the new President that the brigade of exile troops was ready to invade Cuba. CIA officials predicted that thousands, perhaps millions, of people inside Cuba would join the rebellion as soon as the exiles landed on Cuba's beaches. President Kennedy was led by the CIA to believe that the enemies of Castro would overthrow the bearded ruler and end Communism in Cuba.

So the President of the United States ordered the daring mission to begin.

THE BAY OF PIGS

Early on the morning of April 15, 1961, eight planes flew over Cuba. They bombed three airfields, destroying some aircraft on the ground, killing seven persons, and injuring forty-four others. The planes had the markings of the Cuban Air Force, so that people who saw them would think they were flown by Cuban pilots rebelling against Castro. Actually, the planes were made in the United States, painted with Cuban symbols by the CIA, and flown from Nicaragua by Cuban exile pilots.

President Kennedy was told that the raids had destroyed Castro's small air force. This was in fact not true, but the President decided to cancel a second air strike that had been scheduled to occur on April 17, the same day that the invasion force stormed Cuba's shores.

The exile brigade, transported and supplied by ships of the U.S. Navy, landed on the swampy coast by the Bay of Pigs in southern Cuba. Castro personally organized a powerful counterattack that ended the invasion attempt within forty-eight hours. Of the 1,500 invaders, over 100 were killed, and nearly 1,200 were captured and jailed as prisoners. Moreover, the Cuban people failed to rise up against Castro, as the CIA had predicted. Instead, most Cubans united behind their ruler, and Castro's hold on the island was even stronger than it had been before the ill-fated invasion.

The Bay of Pigs mission turned out to be a humiliating defeat—and a dreadful mistake—for both the exile soldiers and the United States government which had backed their futile effort. The attack drove Castro into an even tighter alliance with his new Soviet friends. And, for the first time, Castro now publicly proclaimed that he was a "Marxist-Leninist Communist."

Castro frequently charged that the CIA was plotting to assassinate him. These charges were denied by the CIA. But many years later, in 1975, a Senate committee investigating undercover activities of the CIA discovered that this agency had in fact been involved in attempts to murder Castro between 1960 and 1965. All of these plots against Castro's life failed. Some people, however, believe that Cuban officials who may have known about these plots sought revenge against the United States and possibly played a part in the assassination of President Kennedy in November 1963.

THE MISSILE CRISIS

A grave threat of war occurred in October 1962, when United States U-2 planes photographed missile sites that the Soviets were building in Cuba. Premier Nikita Khrushchev of the Soviet Union claimed that the missiles in Cuba would be used only to defend the island. But President Kennedy feared that Cuban missile sites would be capable of launching nuclear strikes against many cities in the Western Hemisphere. The United States, he concluded, must take swift, decisive action to prevent Cuba from having such dangerous weapons.

President Kennedy's military advisers suggested bombing Cuba and invading the island with a force strong enough to drive Castro from power. But the President feared that this strategy might cause the Soviet Union to help defend Cuba. So he decided on a more cautious approach. On October 22, he addressed the nation on television and solemnly announced that the United States was imposing a naval blockade of Cuba. All ships bound for Cuba would be stopped and inspected, and those carrying missiles would be turned back.

For seven grim days the world waited, on the brink of a possible nuclear war between the two most powerful nations. Each day tension increased as missile-laden Soviet ships drew nearer to the blockade. Would these ships try to run the blockade? Would they then be fired upon? Would the waters around Cuba be the place where World War III began?

Finally, Premier Khrushchev backed down. He promised to stop arming Cuba with missiles if the United States pledged not to attack Cuba. President Kennedy agreed to this proposal. The missile-bearing ships returned to Russia, and the United States removed its blockade of Cuba.

Castro was furious at Khrushchev for giving in to the United States and stripping his country of missiles. But people throughout the world were relieved that nuclear war between the United States and the Soviet Union had been narrowly averted.

CUBA AND OTHER COUNTRIES

Castro was determined to spread his revolutionary movement to other Latin American countries. He denounced the "imperialist" United States as the enemy of progress and urged nearby countries to overthrow their governments and follow Cuba's path to Communism.

The United States was greatly disturbed by Castro's attempt to export his Revolution. Large numbers of people throughout Latin America were very poor, and it was feared they might turn to Communism if it promised them a better life. To challenge the appeal of Communism, President Kennedy in 1961 launched a bold new plan for Latin America called the Alliance for Progress. Over a ten-year period this plan called for the United States to spend $10 billion for aid to the poverty-stricken Latin American countries. Cuba bitterly attacked the Alliance for Progress, but it was overwhelmingly approved by delegates from the other Latin American countries at a conference of the Organization of American States. These Latin American governments again lined up behind the United States when they voted in 1962 to expel Cuba from the OAS.

In the early 1960s Castro was accused of supporting rebel movements in several Latin American nations. When it was proven in 1964 that Castro had supplied arms to guerrilla fighters in Venezuela, all the OAS nations except Mexico ended trade and diplomatic relations with Cuba. Che Guevara, Castro's close friend and supporter, became an important spokesman for revolution in Latin America. In 1965, he resigned his posts in the Cuban government to work for rebel causes in other lands. In moving to Bolivia, he hoped that many peasants there would join his movement to overthrow their government. But, in 1967, Guevara and most of his followers were captured, and the guerrilla leader from Cuba was executed by Bolivian army officers.

CUBA AND THE
WORLD SINCE 1970

Shortly after the death of Che Guevara, Cuba began relaxing its efforts to revolutionize other Latin American countries. Castro faced severe economic problems, and he needed more customers to buy Cuban products. He hoped to reopen those Latin American markets that had been closed to Cuba since 1964.

In the early 1970s, nine Latin American countries reestablished diplomatic relations and trade with Cuba. In 1975, the Organization of American States voted to end its diplomatic and economic boycott of Cuba. The United States was one of the countries that voted to lift the OAS boycott, but it still continued its own trade embargo of Cuba.

Castro was pleased with this action taken by the OAS, but he refused to let Cuba rejoin the organization because he claimed it was dominated by the United States. The Organization of American States, contended the Cuban dictator, was a "shameful alliance between the shark and the sardines."

Just as Cuba had been involved in the affairs of Latin American countries in the 1960s, it became involved in revolutions and civil wars in Africa in the 1970s.

The African country Angola had been a colony of Portugal until 1975. On the eve of its independence, three separate nationalist groups struggled to gain control of the new government. Two of the groups were believed to be friendly to the United States. The third group, called the Popular Movement for the Liberation of Angola, was supported by both the Soviet Union and Cuba. The Soviet Union supplied these Angolan Communists with about $300 million worth of military equipment. Cuba sent about 12,000 troops to Angola, some by airlifts and others by ships. With this aid from Cuba and the Soviet Union, the Popular Movement won the civil war in Angola.

Cuba in 1979 had far more troops stationed in Africa than any other foreign country. It was estimated that there were 20,000 Cuban soldiers in Angola, 17,000 in Ethiopia, and smaller military units in twelve other African nations.

WILL CUBA AND THE UNITED STATES BE FRIENDS AGAIN?

Ever since 1959, the year of Castro's rise to power, Cuba and the United States have treated each other as enemies. In the 1970s, however, both countries took some small but important steps in the direction toward restoring better relations.

Castro is very anxious for the United States to end its trade embargo against Cuba. He wants to sell much of Cuba's sugar and other products to the United States, and buy badly needed machinery, and food products. Many companies in the United States would like to have Cuba as a customer, too.

President Jimmy Carter in 1977 announced the end of restrictions on United States citizens visiting Cuba. The Castro government prepared for a thriving tourist trade expecting many visitors to come each year from the United States. Winter is the most popular season for Americans to vacation in the Caribbean, since they can escape from cold weather at home and enjoy the warm, balmy climate of a tropical island.

For the first time in many years high-ranking United States officials met with Cuban officials in Havana in 1977. Delegates from the two countries signed an agreement that permitted Cubans to fish in waters near the United States.

Another step toward setting up normal diplomatic relations between the two countries was taken on August 31, 1977, when Cuba opened a government office in Washington, D.C., and the United States opened a similar office in Havana. Cultural exchanges between the two nations have also been developing. In 1977, a basketball team composed of two South Dakota college squads went to Havana to play two games against a team made up of Cuban all-stars. (The Cubans won both games.) The following year the Cuban National Ballet was invited to perform in the United States.

Still, there are some difficult problems to overcome before Cuba and the United States can be close friends again. Castro has often said that it is impossible for his country to have normal relations with the United States until its entire trade embargo against Cuba is lifted. Another matter to be settled is who will control Guantánamo Bay. The United States wants to keep it as a naval base; Castro wants it returned to Cuba. Also, the United States would like Cuba to loosen its ties with Russia, but Castro refuses.

The most serious obstacle to improving relations between the two nations is Cuba's involvement in Angola, Ethiopia, and other African countries. Both President Gerald Ford and President Jimmy Carter have stressed that Cuban interference in African affairs casts a dark shadow over all the efforts to strengthen United States–Cuban ties.

Another issue of great concern to President Carter has been Cuba's failure to guarantee the human rights of its people. Before the Cuban military buildup in Africa in 1977, President Carter declared, "The main thing that concerns me about Cuba is the human rights question—political prisoners and so forth."

In December 1978, Castro announced he would release about 3,000 political prisoners if the United States would accept them as refugees. The United States agreed and in 1979 began receiving about 400 political prisoners each month.

But relations between Cuba and the United States worsened in September of 1979 when Cuba hosted the Sixth Conference of Nonaligned Countries. Castro used this conference as a forum to lash out furiously at U.S. policies.

Also in September 1979, the United States government announced it had detected two to three thousand Soviet combat troops stationed in Cuba. Many Americans were disturbed by this news. President Carter addressed the nation on television, and promised that the U.S. would come to the aid of any Latin American nation that might be threatened by a Soviet or Cuban armed attack.

THE GOVERNMENT
OF CUBA

Shortly after he seized control of Cuba, Castro promised his people that there soon would be democratic elections to elect government officials. He also promised the people that they would have a voice in creating a constitution for the revolutionary government. But year after year passed, with no elections and no constitution. Finally, in 1976, a constitution was written by the Communist leaders and submitted to the people. They voted to approve it, but in fact had little choice, since they were not allowed to debate or to change any of its provisions.

The 1976 constitution provides for a somewhat different form of government than had existed before. At the local level, all citizens sixteen years of age and older may vote to elect the members of municipal assemblies. The nomination of candidates for these assemblies are made by the Committees for the Defense of the Revolution, which are the local Communist organizations in every community. Any citizen may run for office, but no campaigning is allowed, and all candidates must be acceptable to the Communist party.

There are about 170 municipal assemblies in Cuba. They

are permitted to make some laws for their own local districts. They also elect members of the national legislature of Cuba, which is called the National Assembly of People's Power.

There are nearly 500 delegates to the National Assembly, and they meet twice a year to consider bills and make laws. The National Assembly elects from among its members the thirty-one persons who make up the Council of State, which is the executive branch of the government that carries out public policies. The National Assembly also selects the Council of Ministers, an executive cabinet that supervises the various branches of the government.

At its first session in December 1976, the National Assembly unanimously elected Fidel Castro as President of the Council of State and also President of the Council of Ministers. Castro's enormous power is as great as ever. And the title that best describes the role he plays in Cuba is "the one and only Maximum Leader of the Revolution."

THE COMMUNIST PARTY AND COMMUNIST ORGANIZATIONS

According to the 1976 constitution, the Communist party is the "highest leading force of the society and of the state." It is responsible for setting the major goals and policies of the government. The position of first secretary of the Communist party,

Fidel Castro was host at the Sixth Conference of Nonaligned Countries, held in Cuba in September, 1979.

which Castro also holds, is almost as important as the office of president.

Youth organizations in Cuba train youngsters to become good Communists and conscientious workers in their communities. The Union of Young Pioneers enlists boys and girls between the ages of seven and thirteen. The Pioneers wear uniforms, attend meetings either at school or after school, and go to "patriotic camps" two weeks each year. Leaders teach the youngsters simple lessons about the meaning of Communism and the importance of the Revolution.

At fourteen years of age Pioneers may join the Union of Young Communists. This organization is the training ground to prepare youths for membership in the Communist party. Cubans may become party members when they reach the age of twenty-seven. Nearly all Cuban children are Pioneers, a smaller group are accepted into the Union of Young Communists, and a still more select group become members of the Communist party.

CIVIL RIGHTS

About one-quarter of the Cuban people are blacks, and before 1959 there was much racial discrimination on the island. The leaders of the Revolution pledged they would end this discrimination. All public places were opened to all Cubans. Blacks and whites became integrated in schools, hospitals, the armed forces, hotels, restaurants, and on the beaches. Racial equality was promised in education, housing, and employment.

Discrimination against blacks has been sharply reduced since 1959. However, the high positions in the economy, the government, and the armed forces are still held mainly by white Cubans, while many of the blacks perform manual tasks.

Before the Revolution, Cuban women were denied equal rights with men. They generally stayed home as housewives. Those who did work outside the home were limited in the jobs they could hold. Many were farm workers, maids, or waitresses, and only a small number of women had enough education to be teachers, nurses, and secretaries.

When the Communists came to power, they needed more workers to increase production, so they encouraged women to enter the work force. Free education became available to all, and women started training for professions and occupations that previously had been limited largely to men. By the early 1970s, over one-half of the medical students and about one-third of the engineering students in Cuban universities were women.

In 1975, the Cuban government established a Family Code which states that husbands and wives have equal rights and duties. It declares that both marriage partners have the right to improve their knowledge and follow careers of their choice. The Family Code proclaims that husbands are legally responsible for half the housework and care of the children.

Citizens in democratic nations are so accustomed to enjoying basic freedoms that they sometimes may take them for granted. But people who live under a Communist dictatorship do not share these basic freedoms.

Freedom of speech, for example, is limited in Cuba to speech that agrees with government policies and goals. Freedom of religion is also restricted; the Cuban constitution says that "the law regulates the activities of religious institutions." Freedom of the press, including the right to criticize the government, does not exist in Cuba. The government owns the only newspapers and also the television networks, radio stations, film companies, publishing houses, and even the billboards.

Everything that the media publishes or broadcasts is controlled by the Communist leaders. Books, magazines, newspapers, and motion pictures produced in foreign countries are carefully screened and censored by the government. *The New York Times,* for example, is kept behind closed doors at the José Martí National Library, and Cubans need special permission from the government to read it.

THE CUBAN ECONOMY

The government controls and directs Cuba's economy. It owns and runs all factories, banks, mines, and large businesses, and nearly all of the small businesses. The government also owns more than 70 percent of the farmland. It operates many large state farms, and the workers on these farms are state employees who receive their wages from the government.

After the Communists seized power in 1959, they resolved to make drastic changes in the Cuban economy. They wanted to end their country's dependence on sugar and on the United States. Cuba no longer would have a one-crop economy, Castro declared, and its trade no longer would be controlled by the powerful country to the north.

So the Communist leaders turned their country's resources to a massive plan for building factories and machinery. Their plan was to change Cuba almost overnight from an agricultural country into an industrial country. They believed that Cuba's factories could turn out huge amounts of manufactured products to sell to other nations. When that happened, Cuba could become prosperous without depending on sugar exports.

But this plan for instant industrialization did not succeed. The Cubans did not have enough money to build many factories and buy raw materials, since at the same time they were financing expensive plans for public education, housing, and health. Most of the technicians and skilled workers needed to operate factories had fled the island when Castro took control. Machine parts and replacements, formerly bought in the United States, were no longer available.

In 1962, the Communist leaders sadly admitted that they had failed to make Cuba an industrial nation. So they decided to shift back to sugar production as the country's chief source of income. Within a few years sugar again accounted for over 80 percent of Cuban exports. Between 1965 and 1969 the annual sugar harvests were about 6 to 7 million tons, and Cuba returned to its role as the world's leading sugar exporter.

With much fanfare and publicity, Castro set a goal for Cuba to produce 10 million tons of sugar in 1970. This seemed like an impossible goal, since the previous record harvest had been 7.2 million tons in 1952. But the Maximum Leader believed this target could be reached if every Cuban did his or her part to help with the giant harvest.

In spite of an all-out effort, the 1970 sugar harvest fell far short of the goal, providing only about 8.5 million tons. The Communist leaders were disappointed and embarrassed, even though it was a record high for that date. Even worse, the 1970 production of meat, milk, vegetables, and clothing had dropped due to the enormous effort put into the sugar harvest.

Since 1970, the Cuban government has set more reasonable goals for sugar production. But Cuba can never be sure how much money will be earned from this crop that provides over four-fifths of its export wealth. Some years the growing season has long periods of drought, and at these times the sugar crop is much smaller than usual. Also, the price of sugar on the world market varies greatly from year to year.

Fortunately for the Cubans, the Soviet Union and other Communist countries in Europe have been buying about three-fourths of Cuba's sugar crop and paying much more than the world market price. But the Cuban economy is still as dependent on the sale of sugar as it was before the Revolution.

CUBA'S OTHER INDUSTRIES

For many years Cuba has been famous for its cigars. Next to sugar, tobacco is still the island's most important farm crop. Cultivating tobacco is a delicate process that requires highly skilled workers. This may help explain why the Cuban government has not combined all the small tobacco farms into large state farms. In 1978, over 60 percent of Cuba's tobacco was still grown by small, independent farmers.

Even though the Cuban government does not own all the tobacco farms, it really controls the tobacco industry. The government regulates the cost of plants, supplies, and equipment that the farmer needs, sets the price for tobacco products, and provides the only market for the sale of these products.

Coffee, like tobacco, has long been grown on small farms in Cuba. Most of the coffee growers are still independent farmers who do not work for the state. But while Cuban coffee was important in colonial times, the size of the crop has declined to the point where Cuba now must import most of its coffee.

Communist leaders have turned unused land on the Isle of Pines into vast tracts of grapefruit groves. Rice is another major Cuban crop, and it is usually cultivated on large state farms in low-lying coastal areas. Other Cuban farm products include bananas, oranges, pineapples, potatoes, and beans. It is necessary, however, to import large amounts of food and cotton to meet the needs of the country's growing population.

Cattle raising is another important activity in Cuba. Scientific experiments are being conducted to increase meat and milk production by improving the breeds of cattle. Even so, the supply of meat and milk has not been able to keep up with the demands of the Cuban consumers, and both of these livestock products have to be rationed.

One industry in which Castro can claim great success is fishing. Before 1959, Cuba had only a few small boats fishing in waters near the island. Their total yearly catch amounted to about 20,000 tons. Cuba's fishing fleet today provides about 240,000 tons of fish annually, which is about twelve times larger than the yearly catch before the Revolution. Also, Cuba has become one of the world's leading exporters of lobster.

Mining is another growing industry in Cuba. One of the world's largest nickel ore reserves lies in the northeastern part of the island. Nickel is used in making steel and in other industrial processes. In a recent year Cuba exported about $200 million worth of nickel. The country's income from the sale of nickel is surpassed only by its income from exporting sugar.

Sugar processing accounts for well over two-thirds of the value of Cuba's industrial production. Other important industrial products include textiles, farm machinery, processed foods and beverages, electric power, cement, and paper.

It is doubtful, however, that Cuba will become a major industrial power. Except for nickel, the island lacks the raw materials needed for heavy industries. Cuba does not have large deposits of coal and easily-mined iron ore, or major rivers to furnish a large supply of hydroelectric power. Moreover, Cuba must import nearly all its oil from the Soviet Union.

In spite of all of Castro's boasts about the success of his Communist state, the economy of Cuba is in grave trouble. The country's leaders are attempting to do too many things with the island's limited income. They are trying to pay wages to a huge work force, launch expensive new building projects throughout the island, support the largest military force in Latin America, and fight costly guerrilla wars in Africa. Furthermore, they are providing free education, free medical care, free recreation, and inexpensive housing for every Cuban. The nation simply does not have enough money to accomplish all this. And the plunge in the world price of sugar in recent years makes the economic situation even gloomier.

The chief reason why the Cuban economy is barely kept afloat is the extensive help it receives from the Soviet Union. We do not know the exact amount of money that the Russians have been pumping into Cuba, but it is estimated to be about $8 million a day! This is an enormous price for the Soviets to pay in order to have a Communist ally in the Americas.

Another serious problem is that the Cuban economy is not as productive as it should be. Again and again the country's farms and factories have fallen short of production goals. This is partly because the Communist system has not provided the Cuban people with enough incentives, or motives, to work as hard as they could.

An important Communist principle is "from each according to his ability; to each according to his need." In a Communist state citizens are expected to devote all their energy and ability to working for the state, and, in return, they are entitled to receive from the state all the material things (food, clothing, housing, etc.) that they need.

During the first years of his rule Castro relied mainly on moral incentives to encourage the people to work their hardest.

Rewards such as medals, badges, pennants, and scrolls were given to the most productive workers. Also, men and women were asked to demonstrate their devotion to the Revolution by volunteering for unpaid jobs after their regular working hours and on weekends.

Some of the Cuban workers did what their Maximum Leader requested. They worked hard at their jobs and then volunteered for additional work without pay. But many others grew lazy and often were absent from their jobs. Since they earned the same salary whether they did their work well or poorly, they had little incentive to do their best work.

In 1971, the Cuban government had to make a new law against "loafing" on the job. Anyone who broke this law could be imprisoned for up to two years, during which time he or she would be forced to do productive work. Later, in the 1976 Constitution, the principle was changed to read: "from each according to his ability; to each according to his work."

WAYS OF LIFE IN COMMUNIST CUBA

Before the Revolution, Cuba, like most other Latin American countries, had two social classes—a small group of wealthy people and a large group of poor people. When the Communists took over the Cuban government, they promised that Cuba would become a classless society in which all citizens would share the same standard of living. This promise has not yet been fulfilled. Some Cubans, such as government officials and doctors, have a much higher standard of living than other citizens.

It is true, however, that the living conditions of the average Cuban workers, especially in the rural areas, have improved greatly since 1959. Today they enjoy better food and clothing and also the benefits of free education and free health services that they were denied before the Revolution.

Housing has not improved as dramatically as other living conditions. Large numbers of farm families still live in the same kind of thatched-roof *bohíos,* or huts, that their ancestors lived in centuries ago. Many other Cubans now live in apartments that the government has been building on a massive scale. There is still, however, a serious housing shortage on the island.

Dwellings often are very crowded, with children, parents, grand-parents, uncles, and aunts all sharing the same quarters. There also are frequent shortages of water and electricity. Most apartments and houses have running water only about two hours a day, and often there are blackouts to conserve electricity.

The Communist economy has not been able to supply all the food that the Cubans want, either by producing it at home or buying it from other countries. So the government has to ration most food products, including such basic items as rice, beans, beef, chicken, fruits, coffee, and milk. Even sugar is rationed by the world's largest sugar exporter at the rate of 4 pounds (1.8 kg) per person a month!

Clothing is also rationed in Cuba. A woman usually can buy in a year only one dress or pair of trousers, one blouse and skirt, one pair of dress shoes, and one pair of casual shoes. Once a year men are allowed to buy three shirts or one shirt and one pair of dress trousers, a pair of work trousers, a pair of shoes, and a pair of work boots.

There are few new cars on Cuban streets and highways. Most of the cars are pre-1959 models from the United States. By contrast, government officials and others in Cuba's upper class drive late-model cars imported from the Soviet Union, Italy, and Argentina.

EDUCATION

Before 1959, about one-quarter of the Cuban people were illiterate. Two out of every three school-age children were unable to attend school, either because they could not afford to or because the schools did not exist. In the rural areas among those few who had attended school, nearly 90 percent had not gone beyond the third grade.

After the Communists took over Cuba, Castro proclaimed, "Education is the Revolution." Schools were assigned two important tasks—converting the Cuban population to accept Communism, and teaching the people to perform the jobs that were needed in this new society. But before the schools could reach large numbers of Cubans, the problem of illiteracy had to be dealt with.

In 1961, which was called the "Year of Education," the government launched an extensive campaign to wipe out illiteracy. In that year, huge throngs of literate adults and over 100,000 schoolchildren between the ages of ten and seventeen spread out over the island to teach reading and writing. They were given about ten days training, handed a teaching book, some clothing, a blanket, a lantern, and a hammock, and sent off to educate their illiterate comrades.

The results were astonishing. By the end of 1961 the number of illiterates in Cuba had been reduced from about 25 percent to about 3 percent of the population. The successful literacy campaign had another important effect—it helped unite the Cuban people. Men and women, young and old, city workers and farmers all were caught up in the exciting crusade to bring reading and writing to an entire nation.

Today Cuba has the most extensive educational system in Latin America. From pre-school day-care units to the island's four universities and many vocational schools, all education is free. The largest expense in the government's budget is for education, and schools employ about 10 percent of the Cuban work force. One of every three Cubans is enrolled in educational courses and 90 percent of all Cuban children are attending school.

The most unusual feature of Cuba's educational system is the boarding school. Some of the pupils in primary school and most of the people attended Catholic services, and many of the schools on the island were operated by the Church. Also, the Catholic Church was the only institution that united nearly all Cubans, and it had a strong voice in shaping public opinion.

After the Communists took over Cuba, the role of the Catholic Church changed drastically. Communism opposes all forms of organized religion, so Cuba's new leaders were determined to break the power and influence of the Church. They deported some of the priests and nuns who criticized the government. Others were threatened with arrest if they continued to speak out against Communist rule.

Through the use of state-controlled television, radio, and newspapers, the Communists informed the Cuban population that the Catholic Church was an enemy of the government. Moreover, they seized all the Catholic schools and ordered that religion could not be taught in any school on the island.

Since about 1965, there has been an uneasy truce between the Church and the state. Priests and nuns no longer openly criticize the government; the Communist leaders no longer condemn the Church. The 1976 Constitution even guarantees freedom of religion to every citizen.

The Catholic Church in Cuba, however, is only a shell of what it had been before the Revolution. The number of priests has declined to one-third its former size and the number of nuns to one-tenth. Church attendance has dropped to only one percent of the population. And Cubans are discouraged from being faithful Catholics. They may still marry in the Church, but they also must have another civil ceremony at a government office. They may still attend mass, but this may cost them the chance to become members of the Communist party. And when the work units decide which Cubans deserve to be on a list to buy scarce products, those who are known Catholics are not likely to be included.

SPORTS

The Castro government sponsors an extensive athletic plan to encourage physical fitness and provide recreation for both athletes and spectators. By the mid-1970s about one-quarter of the Cuban people were taking part in sports. These include baseball, basketball, track and field, gymnastics, boxing, swimming, and many other sports.

Baseball is by far the most popular sport on the island. On vacant lots, school playgrounds, and sugar farms, and in stadiums throughout Cuba, baseball is played enthusiastically by thousands of adults and youngsters.

Some of the best Cuban baseball players made their way to the United States, and about 100 Cubans have either played or managed in the major leagues. Recent Cuban stars on United States baseball teams include Luis Tiant, Tony Perez, Mike Cuellar, José Cardenal, Tito Fuentes, and Bert Campaneris. One promising Cuban pitcher who was observed by a scout for an American League team in the late 1940s was Fidel Castro. Even today the Maximum Leader is Cuba's number one baseball fan, and when he goes to games he often bats or tosses a few balls for the crowd.

THE ARTS

While the Cuban Communists can point with pride to their impressive achievements in education, health, and even sports, the arts have suffered severely since the Revolution. Artistic expression is narrowly restricted and tightly controlled by the Cuban government. Artists—whether they are painters, musicians, or writers—are not free to express their own true feelings. Their work, like everything else in Cuba, must be acceptable to the Communist dictatorship.

When Castro assumed power, many of Cuba's best artists went into exile, moving to other countries where they could work in freedom. Others stayed, and some became loyal Communists.

Popular art for the masses has been linked by the Cuban government to Communist propaganda. The island is dotted with many attractively designed murals, posters, and billboards that advertise some government motto, such as "Men Die—The Party Is Immortal."

The most outstanding musical group in Cuba today is the National Ballet. Headed by the internationally famous ballerina, Alicia Alonso, the National Ballet has performed before large audiences in many countries including the United States.

Literature has suffered more than the other art forms in Communist Cuba. Since the government controls all the printing presses, the works of novelists, poets, playwrights, and non-fiction writers must conform to the revolutionary spirit in order to be published. An author whose writings criticize the government is known as a dissident writer. If somehow the work of a dissident writer is published, it may lead to the author's imprisonment.

The best known case of a dissident Cuban author involved the poet Heberto Padilla. In 1968, the Cuban Writers' Union gave its annual award to Padilla for a book of verse he had written. But Padilla's poetry included some criticism of the Revolution, and it was savagely attacked in the official magazine of the Cuban armed forces. Padilla was sent to jail for offending the government, and he was not released until he publicly confessed that the ideas expressed in his poetry were false.

Many important authors outside Cuba wrote letters and articles protesting Padilla's imprisonment and forced confession. But Castro was not swayed by their appeals that Cuban authors should be free to express their ideas. Instead, he tightened controls on what could be published in his country.

Like all other dictators, Castro refuses to let anyone in Cuba criticize him or the way he rules his small island.

FOR FURTHER READING

Baum, Patricia, *Cuba: Continuing Crisis*. New York: G. P. Putnam's Sons, 1971.

Cuba in Pictures. New York: Sterling Publishing Co., Inc., 1974.

Evans, F. C., *The West Indies*. New York: Cambridge University Press, 1974.

Goldston, Robert, *Cuban Revolution*. New York: Bobbs-Merrill Co., 1970.

Ortiz, Victoria, *The Land and People of Cuba*. Philadelphia: J. B. Lippincott Co., 1973.

Weeks, Morris, Jr., *Hello, West Indies*. New York: Grosset & Dunlap, Inc., 1971.

Williams, Byron, *Cuba: The Continuing Revolution*. New York: Parents' Magazine Press, 1969.

INDEX

(63)